FOR those who walk with Mother Beach,
seeking her hidden treasures.

deepest gratitude to Ron, Oshie, Rania, Kathleen, Anne, and Leap

The illustrations for this book have been rendered in pen and ink and watercolors by Chanda Patel | Mother Beach graphic, created by Greg Straub, is a trademark of Mother Beach | Artistic direction provided by Oshie Merski | Text copyright 2018 by Patricia Merski | Book copyright 2021 by Skeezel Press | Special thanks to Barb Weber Coaching and Jennifer Reed, Relish, Inc. | www.motherbeach.com

ISBN-13: 978-0-9747217-2-9
Library of Congress PCN: 2019942450
Printed in The United States of America
FIRST EDITION 2021

 SKEEZEL PRESS | 2624 Lakeside Drive Erie, PA 16511 | USA | www.skeezelpress.com

Mother Beach

patty merski

ILLUSTRATIONS BY: chanda patel

perhaps a favorite game of mine
an old friend plays with me,
by hiding specks of colored glass
cultured in her sea.

when I take the time to stop my walk
and ask my sandy friend,
"what have you hiding in your lap,
your smile at water's end?"

my gaze surrounds her shores
and soon within my reach,
a splendid piece of smooth, blue glass,
a gift from mother beach!

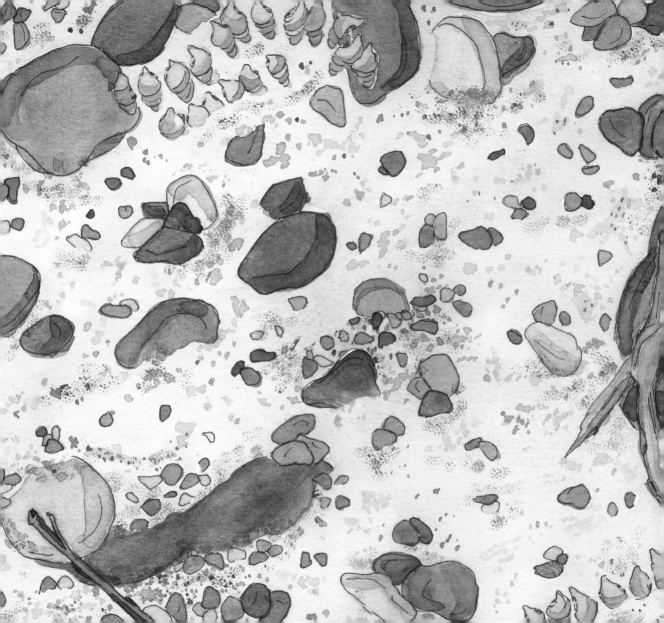

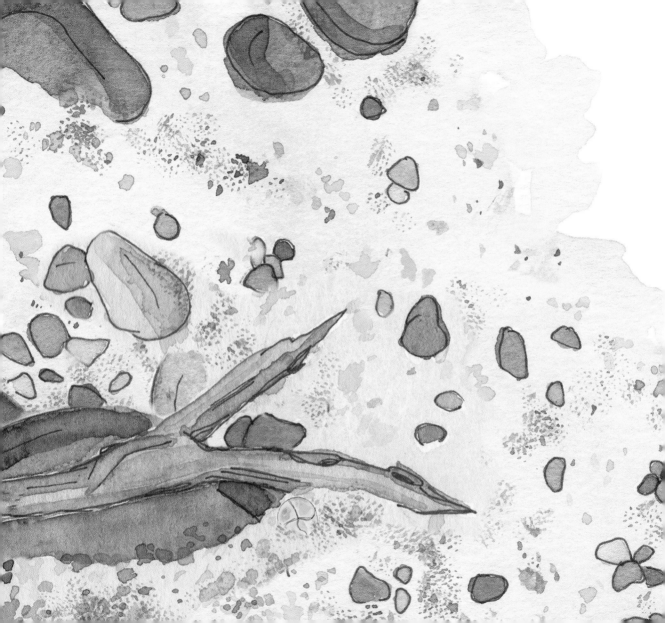

inspired, I take a closer look
move a stone or two,
beside a driftwood lay a marble
hidden in plain view.

in all my years of beach-walking
eyes glued to the ground,
a rare prize such as this
is one I've never found.

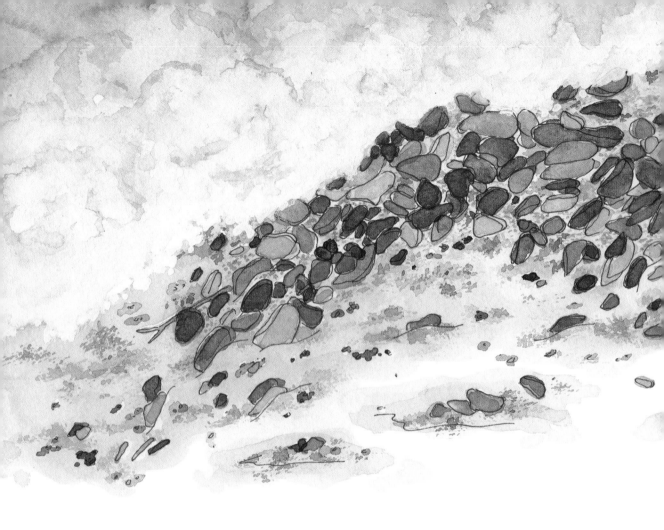

she reveals them oh, so sparingly
these nuggets in her care—
at precisely the right moment
mother beach decides to share.

I kneel and spread a pebbled mound
of stones still wet and clean,
it smells of mossy water…

"ah, two nice chunks
    of green!"

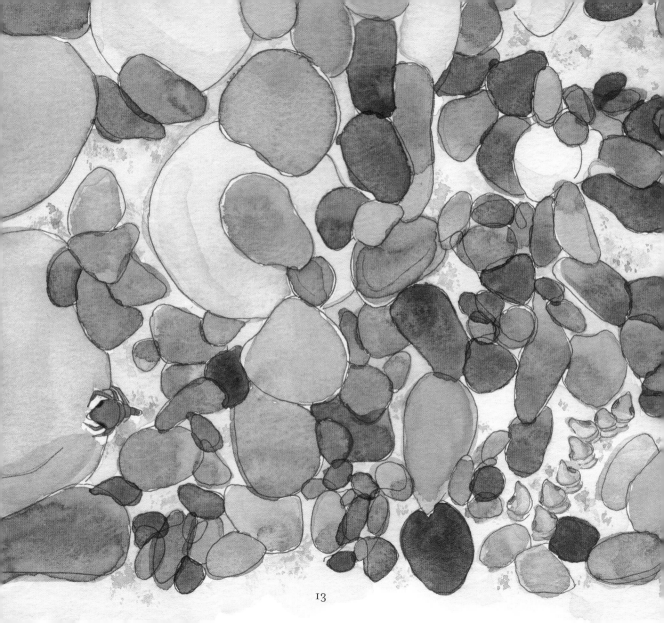

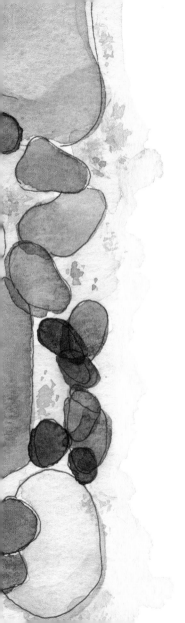

I dig a little deeper
my efforts prove worthwhile,
several colorful shards
are added to my pile.

along the water's edge
this piece of pottery—
a faded wedge from days gone by
worn smooth by sand and sea.

it reminds me of a flower pot
on the cottage window sill,
once brimming with beach treasures
in my mind it sits there, still.

a glint of gold catches my eye
as I continue down her strand,
announcing a chunk of amber
has arrived on new, wet sand.

it has a curvy, floral pattern
once delicate and clear—
perhaps it's from a candy dish
or vase from yesteryear.

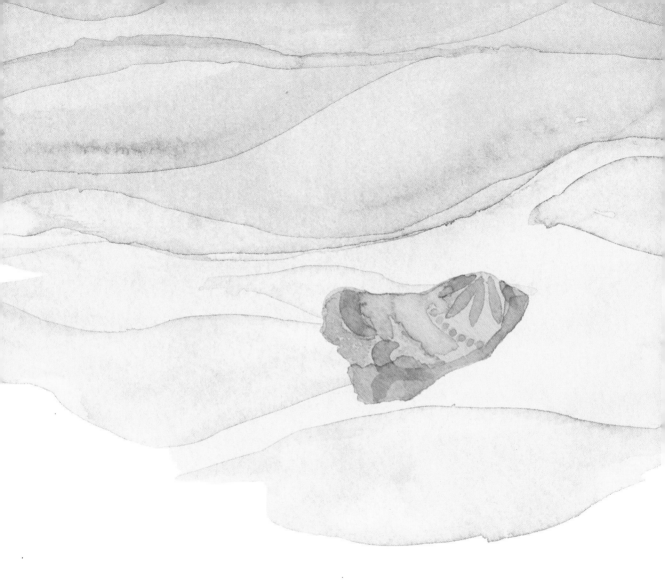

broken in another place
and weathered in her sea,
as if each lovely treasure
was designed just for me.

I wonder how
  she fashions them
mother beach never tells,
etched in rocky waters
tumbled in her swells…

traveling deep beneath the sea
back and forth they go,
mother beach herself, directing
this never-ending flow.

I come across a bed of shells
in scattered clumps and trails,
tiny spirals and conical shapes
the empty homes of snails.

I recall stringing these delicate shells,
strands fit for a Queen...
mother beach's way of showing
not all her gems are green.

a passerby approaches
examining her find,
she holds a mound of frosted pink,
perfectly refined.

we pause to show our treasures
and nod as if to say,
" mother beach outdid herself "
then continue on our way.

it's almost time for me to leave
somehow I think she knows,
another wave rolls ashore and
curls around my toes.

but mother beach loves
hide-and-seek

she's good for one last play,
just when I think we're finished—
I find a piece of gray.

today I found mostly green
ten shades and sizes each,
I wonder if she felt my heart
rejoice in mother beach.

my pocket is full of time-worn glass
more precious to some than gold…
each unique in shape and size,
each a story to be told.

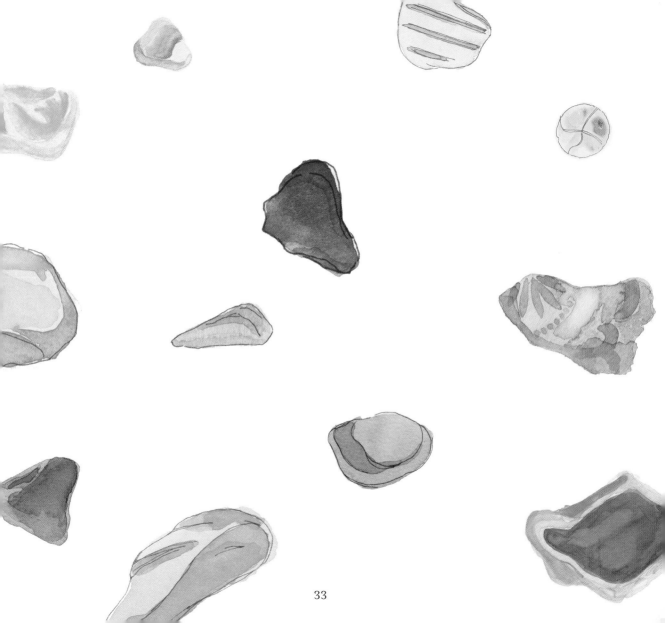

as I walk away my hand caressing
lessons I cannot teach,
I knew my life would soon return
its course to mother beach.

the end.

a few fun facts about beach glass

ON AVERAGE a piece of glass or pottery will spend 30-50 years tumbling before it washes ashore smooth and frosty.

THERE IS A DIFFERENCE between beach glass and sea glass. Beach glass comes from fresh water; it has a different pH balance and is less frosted in appearance than salt water sea glass.

UNTIL RECENTLY, gold was used to color orange and red glass, making these shades some of the rarest to find and claimed by some experts to be one in 20,000! Today, orange or red pieces would likely come from decorative glass such as vintage Avon.

NOT ALL BEACH GLASS is the real deal. To meet growing demands, some artisans will tumble new shards of glass with sand or other corrosives. This man-made beach glass is usually less expensive and looks a bit too perfect.

SEA MARBLES date back to 3000 B.C. Glass marbles were produced in the USA in the 1890s in Ohio, so today, beaches of the Great Lakes remain popular places to find them.

happy hunting!

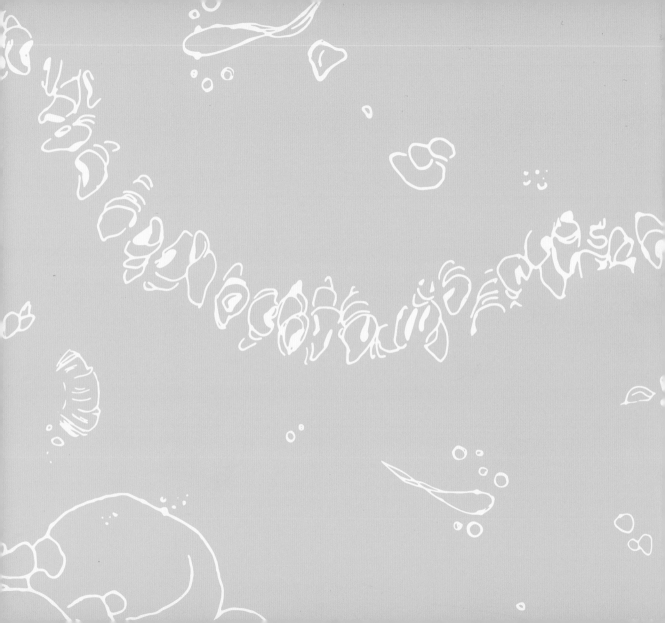